THE GREAT DAYS OF YACHTING

from the Kirk Collection

IAN DEAR

B.T. Batsford Ltd, London

© Ian Dear, 1988
First published 1988

ISBN 0 7134 57538

Typeset by Servis Filmsetting Ltd, Manchester
and printed in Great Britain by
Butler & Tanner, Frome, Somerset
for the publishers
B.T. Batsford Ltd.
4 Fitzhardinge Street
London W1H 0AH

Introduction

The Kirk Collection

When I was approached by Dr Allan Insole of the Isle of Wight Cultural Services Department to write this book, I was intrigued by the fact that at one time there existed a rival to the famous firm of yachting photographers, Beken of Cowes.

William Umpleby Kirk worked from Cowes, too, and, like the first Beken, passed the business down to his son. In fact, William Kirk predated Alfred Beken by quite a few years, and a look at the yachting magazines of the time shows that the firm of Kirk supplied them with as many photographs as Alfred's son, Frank. Although both firms were in existence up to 1939 the Kirk family sold up after the Second World War while Beken carried on and are still, without doubt, one of the best yachting photographers in the world. Their collection of historic yachting photographs has been made famous through the various books they have published, while those of Kirk are almost completely unknown to the general public.

William Umpleby Kirk was born in Hull in 1844. When he was 13 his interest in photography was aroused by seeing his schoolmaster dabbling in the new art. He was then living at Market Weighton, a small market town at the foot of the Yorkshire Wolds. With the help of an article in a boys' magazine he made himself a rudimentary camera and, as no photographic supplies were available in his home town, obtained the necessary collodion and other 'wet plate' materials from York. It was, however, another 15 years before he took up photography seriously, by which time his skills were in such great demand that he became the town's first full-time professional photographer. Later he moved to Waltham-stow, where he lived and worked for several years, before moving to Cowes at the end of the 1870s. He took over number 67 in the High Street, selling general fancy goods and photographic views.

Royal Patronage

Kirk had a studio apart from the premises that was near the end of a garden abutting the sea, where the Island Sailing Club now is. It was here that he carried out his first experiments in yachting photography, a favourite subject being Queen Victoria's yacht, *Alberta*, which passed frequently and at the right distance. He soon found that the camera shutters of those days were not fast enough and fashioned some of his own out of cigar boxes. He made several, but found that the simplest – one whose action was accelerated by

rubber bands – was the best, and it was with this shutter that he eventually succeeded, in 1881, in capturing the *Alberta*, almost certainly the first photograph of a steam yacht in motion ever taken in Britain. (Unfortunately, the original plate has been lost and the photograph (No.2) shown here has been reproduced from *The Yachtsman* magazine.)

The photograph was spotted in Kirk's window by the Captain of the *Alberta* and there appeared in the *Isle of Wight Herald* of 3 September 1881 the following announcement: 'INSTANTANEOUS PHOTOGRAPHY. On the occasion of the Queen's last visit to Osborne, Mr W.U. Kirk, photographer, whose works, by his instantaneous method, have gained him considerable repute, photographed the Royal yacht *Alberta* when steaming into the harbour at a speed of ten knots with Her Majesty and suite on board. The view so taken has since been exhibited to the Queen, and Her Majesty, we are glad to say, was very much pleased with it. We congratulate Mr Kirk on his success.'

In the same year William Kirk succeeded in capturing sailing yachts in motion – the glass plate of this does still exist – and started taking more and more yachting pictures, first from the shore then, with the camera mounted on a stand, from other yachts. He tried many devices for keeping his camera level yet movable, one of which was to suspend it from a boom. In 1896, he had a narrow escape when he and one of his sons were run down by Lord Iveagh's schooner, *Cetonia*, while out photographing a race, but William went on to reach the grand old age of 84.

All three of his sons became photographers: Alan, the eldest, branched out on his own, while Ernest and Edgar stayed with their father. Ernest retired in 1916, leaving Edgar to carry on after William's death in January 1928. Edgar built up the business well, obtaining – as his father had – Royal Patronage. He was invited regularly aboard the Royal Yacht to photograph various members of the Royal Family, several of whom appear in this book. He died in 1949.

This, briefly, is the history of a distinguished family of yachting photographers whose name is known to anyone who has an interest in old yachting photographs. But the story of what happened to the vast Kirk collection of glass plates is equally interesting.

The Photographic Plates are rediscovered

In the winter of 1976 a photographic expert was asked by the Director of Cultural Services for the Isle of Wight to examine a thousand glass plates which had belonged to Kirk and had come into the possession of the department. Many were of poor quality and most had to be restored.

Since then, however, the Cultural Services Department has been able to acquire triple the number of glass plates and the new acquisitions, unlike the earlier ones, were mostly in mint condition. It took a great deal of time to go through these, but once I done so it became obvious that though it was vast and unique collection it was far from being comprehensive. There were, for example, many plates missing from the period immediately preceding the First World War. Investigating further I learnt from various sources that there were still more Kirk plates in existence.

It was then I had the pleasure of meeting Mr G.R. Wells who lives at East Cowes. Mr Wells, now in his eighties, has lived on the Isle of Wight since he was a young boy, knew the Kirk family well, and worked in Cowes at various trades, including that of portrait photographer. During the Second World War Edgar Kirk moved to Wales, and in 1946 he sold his plates and some of his equipment to Mr Wells, assigning to him the copyright in all his work. Mr Wells filled up eleven apple crates with glass plates and took them from Kirk's studio. However, a large quantity of plates remained on the premises and over the years these fell into the hands of various people, including another Cowes photographer, before they were bought by the Cultural Services Department.

Mr Wells kept the Kirk plates and equipment for many years, but never found the time to exploit them commercially. He even used some of the 12 by 10 inch glass plates to repair his greenhouse! At the end of the 1960s he sent some of the plates and all of the equipment to auction at Christie's and, unfortunately, these can no longer be traced. However, Mr Wells did decide to keep about a thousand of the best glass plates and over the years sold framed prints of a few of them in Cowes. Mr Wells kindly allowed me to look at what remained in his possession and, luckily, they included many from the missing period before the First World War. Over 20 of his plates appear in this book, the remainder, with one or two exceptions, coming from those in the possession of the Isle of Wight Cultural Services Department.

There must still be quite a number of missing plates. The really early ones were doubtless destroyed in a fire that took place on William Kirk's premises in the High Street, Cowes, in 1885. Certainly there is very little in either collection that predates the mid-1890s and the pre-1914 examples tend to be from certain years – 1895, 1896 and 1911, for instance. The post-war collection is much more complete, but even here there are gaps. What remains, however, is a unique collection that charts the development of yachting over four of its most beautiful and interesting decades.

THE GRAND YEARS OF YACHTING

The decades during which the Kirk family worked as yachting photographers coincided with some of the greatest, and grandest, years in the sport. Before William Kirk's first efforts at photographing yachts under way, the sport had been poorly governed and was pursued by very few. The Yacht Racing Association (later the Royal Yachting Association) had been founded only a few years previously, in 1876, and it was not until 1881 that it introduced a new rating rule to improve yacht design, which had for years produced vessels with far too narrow a beam. The same year the Royal Yacht Squadron, which had presided over earlier efforts at organizing the sport and had introduced different rating rules, reluctantly agreed to join the Association. From that date the popularity of yacht racing grew rapidly.

The Sail Area Rule

In 1887, the Yacht Racing Association introduced a rating rule that took account, for the first time, of sail area. This encouraged the introduction in 1888 of classes for 10-raters, 5-raters, and 2½-raters, while the 20- and 40-tonners – now called 20-raters and 40-raters – were built in increasing quantities. In 1893, four large cutters were constructed to the new rule, including the famous *Britannia* for the Prince of Wales. During her long life – it more or less spans the era covered by this book –, *Britannia* had no less than seven rigs and her racing record was second to none. In the 569 races in which she took part between 1893 and 1935 she won 355 flags, 231 of them first prizes. Several photographs of her appear in this book (photos 6, 35, 56-8, 80, 96, 97, 100), along with those of her Royal owners, King Edward VII and King George V.

The new rule balanced length with sail area, but no one was quite sure at first whether it was better to have a longer boat with a smaller sail area or, as had been traditional, a shorter boat with a larger sail area. At first, tradition won out, but it was soon found that the longer the boat the faster it went – even though driven by smaller sails – and that excessive overhangs increased this speed still further when the boat was heeled over.

This exploitation of the Sail Area Rule led to the smaller raters increasing in length almost annually and becoming more and more extreme in design – they became known as skimming dishes. As they grew longer – and therefore more expensive – so a new class became established beneath them. Five-raters grew from 20 feet to 34 feet on the waterline and 2½-raters from 16 to 28 feet. One-raters, 1½-raters and ½-raters were then introduced, but these developed even faster than the larger classes with the 1-raters increasing from 10 to 20 feet on the waterline.

Even so, by the standards of the day the smaller raters were looked upon as tiny. 'Nothing can be more delightful than a 2½,' wrote Lord Dunraven who raced in the 5-rater class. 'It is the perfection of racing of its kind; but the absence of any accommodation below is a serious drawback under certain circumstances, especially to a person living at a distance. On a 5 you can change clothes, boil a kettle, and, on a pinch, sleep.' And he was describing a yacht 48 feet long overall, the modern equivalent of which sleeps eight with ease!

By 1895 the 'skimming dish' design began to appear in the larger rating classes, for in that year the American designer Nat Herreshoff produced a 20-rater, *Niagara* (see photo 28), that adopted the plate and bulb keel and shallow displacement that until then had been confined to the smaller classes. The same year, Lord Dunraven, an amateur, designed a 20-rater called *Audrey* (see photo 8) along the same lines, and created the only real opposition *Niagara* had that season.

Linear Rating Rule: 1896

These increasingly extreme designs – especially those of Sibbick, who specialized in small raters – led to the downfall of the Sail Area Rule and, in 1896, it was replaced by the Linear Rating measurement system devised by Froude. This took into account not only a yacht's

length and sail area but also its beam and girth, and resulted in a rating approximately the same as the length of the yacht being measured. Thus, one that was 52 linear rating was about that length on the waterline and became known simply as a 52-footer instead of a 20-rater under the previous rule or a 20-tonner under the tonnage rule that had been introduced in 1881.

The 1896 season was successful, but in the long run the Linear Rating Rule failed to please the owners of the biggest yachts and there began a long decline in first-class racing. The new rule also failed to stop the proliferation of extreme designs in the smaller classes and it became difficult to keep a boat more than a season without it becoming outclassed. In 1900, therefore, the formula was altered to put a very heavy penalty on hollow sections in order to counter the 'skimming dish' design and encourage a roomier type of yacht.

One-Design Classes
As an antidote to these rapid changes in design an entirely new form of yacht racing was evolved – One-Design Class racing, which started with small boats but later included yachts up to about 24 tons. It was started in 1896 with 8-ton yachts that were built on the Solent and were called the Solent One-Design Class. One-Design racing took off in a big way and some of the classes introduced before 1914, like the *Redwing*, are still racing today; while others, like the *Sunbeam Solent*, were introduced after the First World War. A selection of them are reproduced in this book (photos 11, 22, 23, 63, 75, 84).

Despite its lack of popularity in the largest class, the first Linear Rating Rule remained in force until a second one replaced it in 1906, though this was almost immediately superseded by the introduction of the International Metre Rule in 1907.

Ocean racing
While the sport of regatta racing was slowly evolving during the final decades of the nineteenth century, a new one was developing that was eventually to overtake it in popularity. Coastal races between large cruising yachts had been taking place throughout Queen Victoria's reign and the first Round Britain race was held to celebrate the Queen's Golden Jubilee in 1887. The first ocean race to be held on a regular basis was the 300-mile Dover–Heligoland event, introduced by the German Kaiser in 1897 to celebrate the Queen's Diamond Jubilee. It took place every year (except in 1901) until 1908 and gave yachtsmen a foretaste of ocean racing as we know it today.

Other races were held across the North Sea in the early part of the twentieth century, but it was not until 1925 that ocean racing really took off with the inauguration of the Fastnet Race in that year leading to the founding of what is today the Royal Ocean Racing Club. All the yachts that took part in these early races were ordinary cruising yachts, but those that took part in ocean racing after the First World War were far smaller than those that took part at the turn of the century. The term 'ocean racer' was quite unknown at that time and, in fact, it was not until 1935 that a yacht was built specifically to the RORC rule that governed the new sport.

American yachtsmen were much quicker off the mark in designing fast, seaworthy yachts to tackle the ocean courses. Their yachts started to appear in the Fastnet from 1926 – there is a rare photograph of the schooner *Primrose IV*, the first American yacht to enter the race, in this book (photo 64) – and they won it in 1928 with *Nina*, in 1931 and 1933 with *Dorade* (photo 86) and in 1935 with *Stormy Weather*. They also defeated any British yacht that took part in the Bermuda race during the 1920s and 1930s. The only British winner of the Fastnet during the 1930s was *Bloodhound*, which won in 1939, but her rig, deck fittings and interior were American designed.

The International Rule

In 1907, 13 European countries adopted the International Rule. The formula was not all that different from the one it succeeded and was introduced to increase internal accommodation and to discourage the flare and long overhang of the bow. Once more racing yachts were designated differently and now became – to name the most popular – 6-metres, 8-metres, 12-metres, 15-metres, 19-metres and 23-metres. In the Solent, where Kirk took all his photographs, metre class yachts of practically every size – including 5-metres, 7-metres and 10 metres – were built and raced soon after the introduction of the new rule. It is interesting to note, however, that the most popular modern survivor of the metre boats – the 12-metres – did not appear in the Solent until 1910 (having until then only raced on the Clyde and abroad), and a class of them was not established there until 1923. The earliest 12-metres were shorter on the waterline than those that raced for the America's Cup today, but their sail area was very much larger. However, when the International Rule was revised in 1920 a penalty was put on excessive sail area, which hastened the introduction amongst the larger classes of the Bermudan rig, a rig that had already been adopted in the 6-and 8-metres classes by 1914.

The British–American Cup

The Americans did not accept the International Rule at first but continued to build to their own Universal Rule which, unlike the International Rule, did not penalize a yacht's sail area if her length was increased, provided the displacement was also increased. Slowly, however, the Americans became more amenable to adopting the International Rule and one of the main factors in their doing so was the inauguration in 1921 of the British–American Cup. Team racing was something quite novel in the yachting world, but the idea behind it was to bring not only the yachtsmen of the new and old worlds closer together, but also the designs of their yachts.

Some hard negotiations took place and at one time the Americans agreed to build 6-metres, provided the British built to the American equivalent – the R-class – for the return match the following year. However, when it was pointed out that British boats built to an American rule would have no value in Europe once the races had been completed, the Americans sportingly agreed that the series should be permanently sailed in 6-metres. Three series of team races were held between the wars, and Kirk recorded several of those that took place in the Solent (see photo 82).

The America's Cup

Once introduced, the 6-metres became popular in the United States and during the 1920s 12-metres were also introduced as a class. But at first the America's Cup continued to be a law unto itself with both sides building to the maximum size allowed (90 feet on the waterline) without regard to the rating rules springing up on both sides of the Atlantic. It was under these rules that Sir Thomas Lipton challenged with three of his *Shamrocks*, in 1899, 1901 and 1903. When he could not obtain agreement from the Americans to build to a more reasonable size he built himself a 23-metre, which was also called *Shamrock* but was not numbered. Then, just before the First World War, Lipton's fourth challenge was agreed upon, with both yachts being built to the Universal Rule on a waterline length of 75 feet. This led to America's Cup yachts of the 1930s being built to the rule's J-class – that is, yachts built between 76 and 87 feet on the waterline. This in turn resulted, after 1930, in parts of the Universal Rule being adopted by the largest class of yacht racing in the British regatta circuit, which was colloquially known as the 'Big Class'.

The J-class

In 1930, Lipton challenged for the fifth and final time with the J-class *Shamrock V*, but fared no better than he had done on previous occasions.

The Big Class racing in the British regatta circuit that summer consisted of *Candida*, *Astra*, *White Heather II*, *Shamrock V*, *Lulworth*, *Cambria*, *Westward* – and, of course, the King's *Britannia*. At the end of that year all except *Lulworth*, *Cambria* and *Westward* were altered to conform with parts of the Universal Rule, and there followed seven years of racing between them the likes of which has never been seen since. In 1933 the Big Class was joined by the J-class *Velsheda* and the following year by the America's Cup challenger *Endeavour*. In 1935, the apogee of Big Class racing in this country, the American J-class cutter *Yankee* crossed the Atlantic to race for the season in the regatta circuit, but after the death of King George V in January 1936 interest in the class waned, despite a second attempt in 1937 at the America's Cup by T.O.M. Sopwith in *Endeavour II*. Instead, owners of Big Class boats reverted to racing in the 12-metres class.

Both Beken and Kirk have captured the J-class in all their glory, and these magnificient yachts are well represented in this book. It is wonderful that a number are still in existence and are being, or have been, restored to their original splendour.

Kirk's Versatility

Kirk was not, of course, interested in taking photographs only of sailing yachts, and his plates of the early power boats and motor boats are especially interesting. In 1904 he attended the first Motor Boat Reliability Trials, which were organized by the Automobile Club in Southampton Water (photos 34a and b). He was also a keen onlooker at the British International Cup power boat races held the same year at Ryde (photos 34c and d). Later, he photographed the remarkable *Maple Leaf IV*, which won the British International Cup just before the outbreak of the First World War (see photo 50).

Hundreds of Kirk plates were also devoted to other maritime subjects: from large steam

yachts – so big that many were armed and put to use as anti-submarine patrol boats during both world wars – to tiny pinnaces; from warships, liners and freighters down to floating bridges and the launching of several ocean-going vessels. He even photographed some of the earliest flying boats, and one of these is included in this book (photo 45). But the natural choice for most of the photographs included here has been the racing yacht; for it is a unique opportunity to see through the eyes of one family of yachting photographers the expansion and development of one of the world's most popular sports.

1. (Left) *William Umpleby Kirk, the founder of the firm of Kirk. The portrait was taken in his studio at Cowes. As no plate survives, it has been copied from an edition of* The Yachtsman *magazine.*

2. (Top) *No plate survives of Kirk's early experiments in taking photographs of vessels in motion. This one of the Alberta in 1881 is taken from* The Yachtsman *magazine and was, apparently, Kirk's first successful effort at photographing a steam yacht under way.*

3. This earliest surviving Kirk glass plate is of the Prince of Wales' 210-ton schooner Aline
*(right), at the start of a race in 1881. The Prince is on board. On the left of the picture, which
was taken by Kirk from the mark boat, is the yawl* Satellite.

4. *The William Fife-designed 20-rater* Thelma *under construction at C. Hansen & Sons, West Cowes, 1894, for Mr A.B. Walker.*

5. *From left to right:* Carina, Isolde *and* Caress *in a 40-rater race held during the Royal Southern Yacht Club regatta, 15 June 1895.* Isole *won by* $4\frac{1}{2}$ *minutes.*

6. *After racing* Thelma *for one season Mr A.B. Walker commissioned Fife to design him a first-class cutter of 170-rating which he called Ailsa. She proved to be a close competitor of the Prince of Wales'* Britannia, *which is seen here just behind Ailsa during a race in the Solent on 15 June 1895.* Britannia *won by 11 seconds, her tenth victory that year in ten starts.* Britannia, *designed by G.L. Watson, was launched in 1893 and had a remarkable racing career that spanned more than four decades.*

7. The 1-rater Tortoise, *owned by Mr Justice Bruce.*

8. *The start of a 20-rater under the auspices of the Royal Southern Yacht Club, 11 June 1895.*
Lord Dunraven's highly successful Audrey, *which he designed himself by making a model of her*
in clay, is nearest to the camera.

9. Norman, *a 5-rater designed by Sibbick for Captain Orr-Ewing, with two serene female passengers just visible.* Norman *had a phenomenal run of wins during the 1895 season. Out of 56 starts Orr-Ewing won 51 first prizes and this photograph shows her with her winning flags. She was the only 5-rater to race in the equivalent Linear Rating class in 1896, the 36-foot class, but was already outdated.*

10. The Kaiser's Meteor II *designed by G.L. Watson to the new Linear Rating system introduced in 1896, which the Kaiser had built specifically to beat* Britannia. *His nephew's competitiveness annoyed the Prince of Wales so much that at the end of the following season he sold his yacht rather than race against him, though he later bought her back. 'Cowes Week', the Prince told Baron von Eckhardstein, 'used to be a pleasant relaxation for me; since the Kaiser takes command it is a vexation.'*

11. The Solent One-Design Philippine, *25-foot on the waterline, owned by Philip Perceval. Out of 50 starts in 1896 she won 46 prizes – 25 firsts, 17 seconds, and 4 thirds. Like all her class, she was built at Messrs White Bros, Itchen Ferry, Southampton. Perceval later changed his name to Hunloke and became famous as the King's Sailing Master, steering* Britannia *to many victories in the 1920s and 1930s.*

12. *An undated plate of the Royal Yacht* Victoria & Albert III *(nearest the camera), and Czar Nicholas'* Standart *in Cowes Roads. The 5,505-ton* Victoria & Albert III *was launched in 1899, but Queen Victoria always preferred her predecessor,* Victoria & Albert II, *a paddle steamer.* Victoria & Albert III *was broken up at the end of the Second World War having been withdrawn from service in 1937. The 4,334-ton* Standart *was built in 1895 and saw even longer service, for she became a minelayer in the Russian navy and was not scrapped until 1963.*

13. 24 Linear Rating class Parrot built in 1896 at Cowes, and seen here in June of that year off the Royal Yacht Squadron, West Cowes. She raced only six times that season and did not win a flag.

14. *An undated plate of shipyard workers at East Cowes, but probably taken during the 1890s.*

15. *With this undated and uncaptioned plate, Kirk has captured perfectly the leisureliness of a bygone age.*

16. *Two of the 30 Linear Rating class,* Petrel *and* Carol, *racing in 1897.* Carol, *designed by Charles Nicholson and built by Camper & Nicholson, had an impressive record that year: 61 starts, 22 first prizes, 13 second prizes, and 3 third prizes, totalling £152 in prize money.*

17. (Top) *Not all Victorian steam yachts were vast and elegant. This is the 214-ton twin-screw yacht* Speedy II, *built in 1896 to a design by Baron Barreto. She was even equipped with electric lighting. This photograph was taken in 1898.*

18.(Right) *The 5-ton cruising yawl* Lady Hermione, *owned by Lord Dufferin, one of the earliest proponents of single-handed sailing. He developed a taste for sailing solo while ambassador in Constantinople, and when he returned to England devoted himself to the task of inventing gadgets that would help the single-handed yachtsman.* Lady Hermione *was so well equipped for this task that it was said Lord Dufferin could even cast his anchor from the cockpit.*

"Persephone" R.S.Y.C.

19. *The 27-ton cutter* Persephone, *built in 1896. Compared to other boats of her era she has the looks more of a Solent rater than a cruising yacht.*

20. The 36 Linear Rating class Endrick. *She was built in 1899 and proved to be one of the most successful in her class that year.*

22. and 23(overleaf). The Solent One-Design class was one of the most popular in the Solent. These little 8-ton craft gave their owners great sport. No. 22 shows them at the start of a race in Cowes Roads in calm conditions while No. 23 is a dramatic photograph of them under way, topsails doused, in heavy weather. Neither plate is dated but the photographs must have been taken 1899 or later as that was the year the bar under the sail number was added.

23. The Solent One-Design class (see page 33).

21. *Another typical small cruising yacht of her days was the 12-ton cutter* New Woman. *She was built at Cowes in 1899, the year this photograph was taken.*

24. In 1901 tea baron Sir Thomas Lipton produced his second America's Cup challenger,
Shamrock II. *She was 89 foot 3 inches on the waterline and 137 foot overall, carrying a sail
area of over 14,000 square feet. She was tuning up in the Solent on 19 May 1901, with King
Edward VII aboard, when her bowsprit carried away, which in turn caused her mast to go over
the side. The races, which the challenger lost 3-0, were delayed a month by the accident.*

25.(Top) *Sir Thomas Lipton's 1242-ton steam yacht* Erin, *which he purchased for $300,000 in 1899. He entertained widely in her during his first three challenges for the America's Cup. During the First World War she became a hospital ship before being handed over to the Admiralty for patrol work in the Mediterranean, where she was later sunk.*

26.(Right) *The 36 Linear Rating class* Girleen *in Cowes Roads, 1901. Note the lady crew complete with straw hat and veil!*

27. *The 4838-ton steamship* Mongolian, *owned by the Allan Line, was used late in 1899 as a troop transport (Transport no. 17) for soldiers fighting in the Boer War.*

28. *In 1895 an American yachtsman, Howard Goulden, brought over a Herreshoff designed 20-rater called* Niagara *and raced her with great success. In 1901 she was bought by a British yachtsman who changed her name to* Japonica *and her rig from cutter to yawl. This photograph of her hauled out at Cowes clearly shows her 'skimming dish' design and plate and bulb keel that up until then had only been used on much smaller yachts.*

29. *The 560-ton auxiliary schooner* Utowana *in Cowes Roads in August 1904. She was designed by British naval architect J. Beaver Webb, but was built in Philadelphia in 1891. In 1902, the Coronation Cup was donated by the Earl of Crawford, a keen yachtsman, who stipulated that it must be raced for by 'auxiliary steam vessels' above 430 tons. The course was across to Cherbourg from the Nab Light, then round the Eddystone Light and back to Cowes.* Utowana *was owned by Mr Allison Armour and was the only fore-and-aft rigged yacht in the race. She won easily, becoming the first American vessel ever to win a British offshore race.*

30. *The 263-ton schooner* Cicely *was designed by William Fife in 1902 for Mr Cecil Quentin and was later owned by Mr Cecil Whitaker. She was a match for any of the other schooners racing at that time, and could easily beat the Kaiser's schooner* Meteor III *also built in 1902 on every point of sailing except reaching.*

31. Germaine, *a typical late Victorian cruising yawl, built by Camper & Nicholson in 1882. Her tender is under tow but would normally have been hoisted on the davits on the port side. The plate is not dated but it must have been taken between 1904 and 1910 as it was during this period that she was owned by Major and Mrs Middleton Robinson. They were members of the Royal Albert Yacht Club whose initials are on the yacht's lifebuoy.*

32. The 52 Linear Rating class Moyana, designed by Alfred Mylne, was launched in 1903 and proved to be a highly successful racing yacht for her owner, Mr J.W. Leuchars.

33. White Heather *(153 tons), the Kaiser's* Meteor III *(412 tons), and* Brynhild *(153 tons) racing in the Solent in 1905.*

a

b

c

34(a). *In July 1904 the Automobile Club organized the first ever Motor Boat Reliability Trials. They were held in Southampton Water, with the aim of persuading both the Royal Navy and the general public that the new fangled internal combustion engine was as reliable afloat as it was proving to be ashore. For ten hours a day non-stop for two days the participating motor boats had to round the course of 9.53 nautical miles as often as they could without breaking down. Most managed to do so but the 40-foot craft pictured here ran into trouble, as can be seen by the gesticulations of the crew and adjudicator. Entered by Messrs Gorham and Manville, it was powered by a 4-cylinder Constatt Daimler petrol engine that pushed it along at a respectable nine knots or more. Unfortunately, however, air entered the water inlet and, though the airlock was cleared by racing the engine, this 'deranged' the clutch and the boat was forced to retire after completing eight circuits.*

(b). *Two more entries for the 1904 Motor Boat Reliability Trials. In the foreground is a 30-foot carvel-built motor boat, belonging to Woodnutt Motor Company and powered by a 2-cylinder 10hp American Long Distance engine; behind it is the sleek, 'slipper-shaped' 25-foot motor boat* Baby *entered by Brooke & Co. of Lowestoft. The larger boat did remarkably well and covered the course on both days without stopping, at an average speed of 7.41 knots, consuming 39 gallons of petrol; for this feat it won the silver medal for its class.* Baby, *which was powered by a 3-cylinder 14hp petrol engine of the owner's design, was not so fortunate as various faults stopped it for 14 minutes on the first day and 13 minutes on the second. Nevertheless, it completed the course on both days at an average speed of 7.82 knots.*

(c). *In 1903 the Harmsworth Trophy (afterwards called the British International Cup) for speedboats was inaugurated. The following year it was held at Ryde and had entries from France, Britain and the United States. Seen here is one of the American entries,* Challenger, *which was powered by two 4-cylinder 75hp Smith and Mabley engines. It was designed by Clinton Crane and had a top speed of about 20 knots.*

(d). Napier II, *seen here at top speed, was another entry for the 1904 British International Cup races. Built and designed by Yarrow & Co. she had two 4-cylinder 90hp Napier engines and was constructed of 16, 18 and 20 gauge steel. Entered by S.F. Edge Ltd,* Napier II *beat the American entry* Challenger *in a preliminary heat but later had to retire because of a leak.*

35. Sorais, *a new 24 Linear Rating class designed by William Fife in 1906, the year this photograph was taken. The lady in the cockpit is almost certainly the owner, Mrs H.G. Allen.*

36. *King Edward VII aboard* Britannia *in 1906. After selling her in 1897 he bought her back in 1902 and used her as a cruising yacht until his death in 1910.*

38. *The 23-metre* Shamrock *slicing through the Solent. She was built in 1908 for Sir Thomas Lipton. The photograph is undated.*

39. The Archduke Karl Stephan of Austria with his family aboard his 766-ton steam yacht Ui, *which was launched at Leith in May 1911. He visited Cowes in September that year, which is when this photograph must have been taken, though the plate is undated. The* Ui *later became the* Sayonara *(see photos 65-9).*

40. *A gunter-rigged 6-metre,* Snowdrop, *racing in July 1911. The 6-metres were the first international class to adopt the Bermudan rig, in 1914. A few still race today.*

41. *These two gaff-rigged 12-metres,* Cintra *(left) and* Alachie, *are a far cry from today's breed of 12-metres. This photograph was taken of them competing in the First European International Regatta at Ryde in August 1911. All the early British 12-metres came fron the Clyde and a 12-metre class was not established in the Solent until 1923.* Alachie *was the outstanding 12-metre of her period. Between 1908, when she was launched, and 1911 she took part in 137 races, taking 43 first and 54 other prizes. The 12-metre class collapsed after 1911 and was not revived until 1923.*

42. (Left) *Mrs Alwyn Foster aboard Lord Howard de Walden's 151-ton steam yacht* Branwen *in August 1911. As can be seen from this and other photographs in this book, women were as keen participants as men during the golden age of yachting.*

43. (Above) *The 15-metre class in the Solent was always more numerous than the 19-metre class. In 1911, the year this photograph was taken of two of them,* Ostara *and* Mariska, *they numbered eight, including the King of Spain's* Hispania.

44. *Only four 19-metres were ever built in Britain. Here are three of them,* Mariquita, Corona *and* Octavia, *racing in the Solent in August 1912. The fourth,* Norada, *can be seen in photo 73.* Mariquita, *owned by Mr A.K. Stothert, headed the prize list in 1912 with 23 firsts out of 30 starts.*

45. *The luxurious accommodation of the Victorian steam yacht is something rarely seen today. This is the cabin of a Miss Squire in the 451-ton* Invincible, *built in 1893. The photograph was taken in 1912.*

46. On 10 August 1912 an early aviation pioneer, Claude Grahame-White, flew his hydro-aeroplane – as the early seaplanes were called – at Cowes. He flew over the yachts at anchor and then circled the Royal Yacht, which had King George V and Queen Mary on board. Finally, he took the plane as close to the Royal Yacht Squadron as he could 'so that the members attending the garden party might have a good view of it'.

47. *This photograph of the magnificent 565-ton, three-masted topsail auxiliary schooner Sunbeam was taken in August 1912. She was owned by Lord Brassey, who had her built in 1874; and in 1876–7 he sailed her around the world, the first privately-owned yacht to achieve this distinction. His wife wrote a book about the voyage that sold millions of copies and is still in print.*

48. Three early 8-metres, Le Jade, Antwerpia IV *and* Ventana, *racing in the Solent in 1912. By 1914 the class had begun to adopt the Bermudan rig.*

49. (Left) *The 380-ton schooner* Margherita *was designed by Charles Nicholson for Mr Cecil Whitaker in 1913, the year this photograph was taken. That season she won every race that she entered except one in the Kiel Regatta.*

50. (Top) *The hydroplane* Maple Leaf IV *in which T.O.M. Sopwith won back the British International Trophy (formerly the Harmsworth Trophy) from the Americans in 1912. He successfully defended the trophy the following year in Osborne Bay against French and American challengers. This photograph was taken in September 1914.* Maple Leaf IV *was powered by two Austin engines, generating 400 horsepower.*

51. (Left) *The Marquis of Ailsa's 40-tonner* Bloodhound *was built in 1874 and raced successfully until 1880 when she apparently became obsolete and was replaced by* Sleuthhound. *However, in 1907, the Marquis acquired her again and, as an experiment, put her into racing condition to see how she would compete with her modern counterparts in the handicap class. The result was remarkable, and between 1909 and 1914 she won 142 prizes, 64 of which were first. Out of 30 starts in 1914, when this photograph was taken, she won 19 firsts.*

52. (Top) *By the 1920s Claude Grahame-White had turned from aviation to power boating. Here is his experimental 45-foot power sledge,* Miss England, *which was built of wood by the Cowes firm of S.E. Saunders in 1921. Though powered by a 24-cylinder Rolls Royce petrol engine,* Miss England *does not seem to have been a great success. This picture was taken on 3 September 1922.*

53. (Left) *The 15-mètre class did not survive the First World War but a few kept racing in the handicap class during the 1920s. This is* Paula III, *designed by Charles E. Nicholson for Herr Ludwig Sanders in 1913. Postwar she was owned by Kenneth Preston, who was given her as a wedding present in 1923, the year this photograph was taken. In 1925 she broke her back in a storm and Preston turned to racing 6-metres, which he did with great success.*

54. (Top) White Heather II, *pictured here off Cowes in August 1924, was one of the first 23-metres ever built and she raced consistently between 1907 and 1932 when she was scrapped by her last owner, Bill Stephenson, who replaced her with the J-class* Velsheda.

55. (Top) *The inter-war period saw a blossoming of small dinghy classes. Here two Yarmouth – or Solent – Sea Birds,* Waterwitch *and* Seamew, *are racing off Yarmouth in August 1924.*

56. (Right) *The 23-metre* Shamrock *kept racing during the early 1920s under the ownership of Sir Thomas Lipton and proved to be highly competitive. This photograph of her was taken in August 1924.*

57, 58, 59. King George V adored yachting as much as his father had. These three photographs, taken during the 1920s, show him aboard Britannia. The photograph in which he is talking to his sailing master, Sir Philip Hunloke, is the only one I have ever seen of the King actually smiling!

58. *King George V aboard* Britannia.

59. *King George V aboard* Britannia.

60. (Top) *The cutter* Lulworth *in the Solent, 5 August 1925.* Lulworth *was built in 1920 as a competitor to the King's* Britannia *and was originally called* Terpsichore. *She was never converted to the J-class and ended her days first as a cruising yacht and then as a houseboat. She is currently being restored to her original condition by her present owner.*

61. (Right) *Modern ocean racing really began with the first Fastnet race, which took place in August 1925. It was won by a 56-foot converted Le Havre pilot cutter,* Jolie Brise, *built in 1913. She went on to win it again in 1929 and 1930, and is still sailing today.*

62. (Top) *The 555-ton motor yacht* Sona, *built for Lord Dunraven in 1922 by Camper & Nicholson. This photograph was taken in 1926 when she was owned by the newspaper magnate Sir William Berry. She was requisitioned by the Admirality in 1939 as an anti-submarine patrol vessel. In 1942 a German bomb broke her back while she was being used as an accommodation ship in Poole harbour.*

63. (Right) *The 152-ton ketch* Cariad II *was built for Lord Dunraven in 1903 to replace a slightly smaller* Cariad *built in 1895. He won the King's Cup in her 1905, 1912 and 1921. This photograph of her was taken in August 1926 when she was owned by Colonel Gretton.*

64. The Seaview Mermaids were one of the earliest one-design classes to spring up in the Solent, becoming established in 1907. They are still raced today. This photograph was taken on 28 July 1926.

65. *The Alden-designed schooner* Primrose IV, *owned by Frederick L. Ames of Boston, soon after the start of the second Fastnet race, 14 August 1926. She lost the race to* Ilex *by a mere 13 minutes 8 seconds on corrected time. Behind her is* Jolie Brise. *This is the only photograph I have ever seen of this, the first American yacht ever to enter the Fastnet race.*

66. *The 766-ton steam yacht* Sayonara *was built to G.L. Watson's design in 1911 for Archduke Karl Stephan of Austria who called her Ui. At the time these photographs were taken, in 1927, she was owned by an American, Anthony Drexel.*

67. Interiors of Sayonara: *the dining saloon.*

68. Interiors of Sayonara: *the main saloon.*

69. Interiors of Sayonara: *the library.*

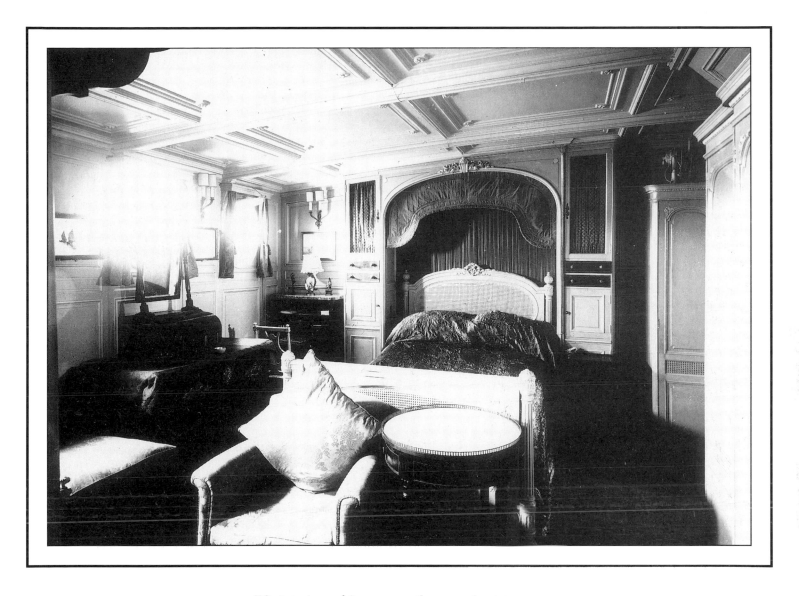

70. Interiors of Sayonara: *the owner's statesroom.*

71. *Two 14-foot Nationals,* Pussyfoot *and* Felix-the-Cat, *racing in an Island Sailing Club race on 28 June 1927. That same year the 14-footers became an International Class and went on to become one of the most popular racing dinghies ever designed.*

72. (Top) *The Alden-designed American schooner* La Goleta, *which competed in the 1927 Fastnet race, one of the toughest ever held. Fifteen started but only two finished,* La Goleta *crossing the line just 42 minutes ahead of* Tally Ho!, *which won on corrected time.*

73. (Right) *The 19-metre* Norada *was designed by Charles E. Nicholson for Mr. F. Milburn in 1911. The 19-metre class was dead by 1914, but* Norada *kept racing in the largest handicap class during the 1920s, as this photograph, taken in August 1928, testifies. She was then owned by Sir Howard Frank.*

74. *The start of the fourth Fastnet, 15 August 1928.* Neptune, *on the left, was a British entry, while* Mohawk *(centre) and* Nina *(right) were both Americans.* Nina, *a 50-foot schooner skippered by Sherman Hoyt, won, becoming the first American yacht ever to take the Fastnet Cup.*

75. *The spectacular 338-ton, Herreshoff-designed schooner, Westward, was built in 1910. She was owned between the wars by one of the era's great characters, T.B.F. Davis. She sailed in the Big Class during the 1920s and was one of Britannia's great rivals. She occasionally raced in the 1930s but was outclassed except in a very heavy blow.*

76. *Several small One-Design classes were started after the First World War. One of these was the Sunbeam Solents, seen racing here on 13 June 1929. The class first appeared in 1923 and they are still a popular class today.*

77. Minnow II, *a typical speedboat of the 1920s.*

78. *Few accidents occurred in Big Class racing, but in 1930 the new 12-metre* Lucilla *was run down by* Lulworth *off Cowes, killing the smaller boat's steward. This remarkable photograph shows the moment of impact, with one of* Lucilla's *crew just visible jumping for safety on to* Lulworth's *bow.*

79. and 80. (overleaf) Two typical cruising yachts of the inter-war period, which illustrate well the change in rigging that brought about the introduction of the Bermudan sail. On the left is the converted Bristol Channel pilot cutter Dyarchy, built in 1901, where the topmast – stowed in this picture – is fidded to the mainmast. Overleaf is the 56-ton cutter Douna, whose topmast has become an extension of her mainmast. This was what became known as the 'marconi' rig – so-called after the early radio masts and their mass of wires. The next step was to make the mainsail and topsail one piece of canvas, and this became the familiar triangular Bermudan sail used by nearly all modern yachts. The Bermudan rig was in use among the smaller metre classes prior to the First World War, but most cruising yachts retained the gaff right up to the Second World War – quite a few still use it today.

80. The 56-cutter Douna *(see page 100).*

81. Lulworth *and* Britannia *duelling on a blustery day in the Solent, 5 August 1930.*

82. Six-metres racing in the Solent for the British-American Cup on 20 July 1921. Four separate series of these team competitions have taken place between the British and Americans between 1921 and 1986, the more recent races taking place in E22s, Solings and Sigma 33s. The British won the first series but lost the next two. A fourth series was started in 1951 which, unlike the others, is to continue in perpetuity. At the present time the score in this series is five matches to the Americans, one to the British, and two ties.

83. (Left) The 23-metre Candida was designed by Charles E. Nicholson for the banker Mr. Herman Andrae. She was launched in 1929 and proved to be most successful. After the 1930 season she was converted to the J-class and raced every year until 1935. She was later converted to a cruising yacht and is now based in the Mediterranean under the name Norlanda.

84. (Top) The 611-ton auxiliary barque Fantome II (ex-Belem), which the Hon. Ernest Guinness bought from the Duke of Westminster in 1921. This photograph was taken in 1930.

85. (Top) The West Solents were another One-Design class that flourished between the wars. This is one of them, Dilkusha, taken on 4 August 1930, a sunny but windy day. She was owned by Col. the Hon. Henry Guest, who raced her very successfully over a number of years.

86. (Right) The 23-metre Cambria was built for the newspaper magnate Sir William Berry (later Lord Camrose) in 1928. She won her first race at Harwich but hardly took a flag thereafter. She was never converted to the J-class and did not race during the 1930s.

87. *The yawl* Dorade, *one of the classic ocean racers of all time. 52-feet overall,* Dorade *carried 1,150 square feet of canvas. She was designed by Olin Stephens who became a legendary postwar designer of ocean racers and 12-metres. With his brother Rod he sailed* Dorade *to victory in the 1931 Fastnet, and Rod won again with her in 1933. Here she is at the start of the 1931 race. It began in a flat calm but became one of the roughest on record.*

88. Shamrock V, *the first British yacht ever to be built to the J-class of the American Universal Rule. She was Lipton's last effort to win the America's Cup, which she failed miserably to do in 1930. She is pictured here in June 1931, after a short bowsprit had been added to enable her to conform to the J-class regulations that governed the Big Class from 1931. In October 1931 Lipton died and* Shamrock V *was bought by T.O.M. Sopwith.*

89. Britannia *in July 1931 with her first Bermudan rig.*

90. *The 23-metre* Astra, *built for Sir Mortimer Singer, the sewing maching millionaire, in 1927. During the 1930s she was owned by Hugh Paul.*

91. The start of an 8-metre race, 7 July 1932, with Severn *(23)*, Deama *(18)*, and Nona *(9)*. The 8-metres were one of the most popular classes in the Solent during the 1930s.

92. (Top) *The 161-ton, Fife-designed schooner* Altair, *built in 1931 for Captain Guy MacCaw. This photograph was taken in squally weather conditions on 1 August 1933.*

93. (Right) *In 1933, Charles E. Nicholson designed a steel J-class cutter for the Woolworth's chairman, Bill Stephenson. She was called* Velsheda, *from the first letters of his daughters' names: Velma, Sheila and Daphne.* Velsheda *is still being sailed today.*

"VELSHEDA"

94. (Top) *The shipping magnate Sir Walter Runciman was a great admirer of Lord Brassey and owned the latter's* Sunbeam *during the 1920s. In 1929 he realized she was worn out and had her broken up. But so great was his attachment to her, and to her original owner, that he had* Sunbeam II, *pictured here, constructed.*

95. (Right) *The J-class* Endeavour, *designed by Charles E. Nicholson for T.O.M. Sopwith's 1934 America's Cup challenge. She was acknowledged to be the fastest J afloat that year, but crew trouble and the sailing skills of Harold Vanderbilt kept the cup in the United States.*

96. *The 799-ton* Vita II *(ex-Argosy), built by Frederick Krupp in 1931. When this photograph was taken, on 8 May 1934, she was owned by T.O.M. Sopwith.*

97. *A J-class start during Cowes Week, 1934.* Candida *is nearest the camera and* Britannia *is on the far end of the line.*

98. (Left) *King George V, Queen Mary and the Duke and Duchess of York aboard the Royal Yacht, 1935.*

99. (Top) *RMS* Queen Mary *passing Cowes Front, August 1936.*

100. T.O.M. Sopwith again tried to win the America's Cup in 1937, this time with the J-class Endeavour II pictured here the previous year. He failed 4-0.

101. (Top) King George V died in January 1936. He left instructions that Britannia *should be* sunk off St Catherine's Point, Isle of Wight. This photograph, taken on 8 July 1936, shows her being towed to her end after being stripped of everything saleable.

102. The Duke of Westminster's Flying Cloud *at the 1937 Coronation Review. At over 200 feet in length she was one of the largest private yachts in the world and the Duke employed the architect Detmar Blow to turn her into a floating palace.*

103. (Top) *The 458-ton* Malahne *was built by Camper & Nicholson in 1937 for the English boss of Woolworths, Bill Stephenson, who also owned the J-class* Velsheda. *Stephenson had three daughters, Velma, Sheila and Daphne.* Velsheda *was from the first two or three letters of their names;* Malahne *from the last two or three.*

104. *The 161-ton schooner* Amphitrite, *designed by Charles E. Nicholson's father, Ben Nicholson, who built her in 1887. This photograph, taken in 1937, shows she was still going strong then. She survived the Second World War and was still in commission in the late 1970s as a German-owned training ship.*

105. (Top) *A group of Bembridge Redwings taken on 4 August 1939. This class was one of the first of the One-Design classes to be formed when 14 were built in 1896. Their sail area was restricted to 200 square feet but there was no restriction on the sail plan. This resulted in some extraordinary experimental rigs, including one that was rigged with an autogyro! The original boats were replaced in 1938. The new ones were slightly longer but with the same sail area.*

106. *It is appropriate to end this book with a picture of the only metre class yachts to flourish postwar – the 12-metres, which have raced for the America's Cup since the second World War. Here are T.O.M. Sopwith's* Tomahawk, Blue Marlin, Evaine *and* Jenetta *during one of the last races in the Solent before the outbreak of the Second World War. The date is 1 August 1939.*

107. *The 41-ton* Latifa, *designed by William Fife Jr and owned by Michael Mason. She was launched in 1936 and was one of the outstanding ocean racers of her day, winning many events both before and after the war.*